Every journey

Begins from

The smallest room

INSIDE

잿빛 손가락 사이로 흘러내리는
초콜릿 세례를 눈물인 양 할짝거리며
귀가를 재촉하는 무리들 사이
혼연히 혼자임을, 절감했던 나날들

Licking the baptism of
chocolate that was
flowing between
pale grey fingers...

Latte & Almond Croissant

Somebody's
Internal feelings
or Vivid storytelling
for somebody

J kaya Lee

Latte Almond Croissant

œuf mollet et miel

꿀을 곁들인 달걀

PART. I
APPETIZER DISH

Meilleur Bonbon de France
nées du fruit de l'amour et du plaisir
Les
Coucougnettes
FABRICATION ARTISANALE
En vente ici
MEILLEUR BONBON DE FRANCE
MAISON FRANCIS MIOT
FRENCH HAUTE GOURMANDISE

Melancholy pink & baked yellow

27th December Mon
am 7:42

Into the small chaos

서랍 속 깊은 곳에서 발견한
낡은 엽서 얼룩에서는
아몬드 크루아상
냄새가 났다
아득하니

8th September Thu
pm 3:26

The scent of almond croissant
comes from ink stain
on a postcard found
in back, back of drawer

Český Krumlov

Latte & Almond Croissant

Crispy choco creperie

재의 수요일이 시작되는 첫날
크레페를 찾아 헤매다

흑설탕 시럽, 꿀이나 잼
초콜릿 스프레드
레몬즙과 슈가파우더
어느 날엔가 직접 졸인
살구 무스를 곁들이면
좋은 꿈을 꾼다는 믿음이 생겼다

15th June Wed, am 11:27
Paris France

18e Arrt
RUE
ROBERT
PLANQUETTE
01 46 06 62 07
LA MIDINETTE
RESTAURANT BAR
CAVE
01 42 54 40 70
G20
SUPERMARCHE
SUPERMARCHÉ

17th June Fri
am 10:13

Ash blonde in Paris

Latte & Almond Croissant

Red brasserie for red wine

생기 없는 버터 바른
빵 한 조각과
질 좋은 포도주 한 잔
그것만으로 완연히
충분하던 한때가 있었다

L'ANNEXE
CAFE RESTAURANT
CAFE
1€
BAR-TAKE-AWAY
BIERE
2€
BAR-TAKE-AWAY
TAKE AWAY
CAFE
THE
CHOCOLAT
SANDWCHES
VARIES
À EMPORTER
BRASSERIE
WiFi

His rye baguette

차곡
차곡 쌓인
호밀밭 흑빵 무더기
텀벙대는 삶의 소음
벌꿀색 콘크리트 담 너머로
흔적없이 여물었다
부스러기 위 우웅웅
날갯짓 소리

22nd June Wed, pm 2:41
Arles France

Latte & Almond Croissant

du Désert
Décoration, composition florales
Mariages – Réceptions

어처구니가 없군
이건 한 마리 비둘기와
코끼리의
결혼이야
프리다Frida의 어머니가 말했다
눈물짓지 마세요, 어머니
그가 매일 나를 다시
태어나게 하는 걸요

Le Tastevi

Charles Rennie
Mackintosh
BIG BOOK

"……크루아상을 데워줄까요?"
이름도 쉬이 찾아보기 힘들 만큼 한갓진
스페인 시골 동네 선술집, 무쇠 프라이팬 위에서
구워져 나온 투박한 크루아상은 너무나도
따뜻하고, 고소하고, 충만한 기운을 머금고 있어
나는 그만 감격해버리고 말았다.
……불가능하다는 사실을 알면서도, 때때로,
그날의 크루아상 한 조각을 사무치게 그리워한다.
에펠탑 전망대보다도 호젓한 무덤가가 더 마음에 들어
오스카 와일드의 비석 위 -누군가의 립스틱 자국-를
혼곤히 쓰다듬고 돌아오던 날들, 멋대로 가져다 붙인
프랑스식 이름과 뜻 모를 글귀들을 그러모아
식물원 입구에서 백스물여덟 발자국 떨어진 나무
옹이 사이에 살풋 쪽시를 끼워넣고 돌아서던 시간들.
나만의 장소에서, 나만의 형상으로,
온전히 나만의 추억으로 남을 희미해진 문신 같은
흔적들을 좇아…… 스쳤던 곳을 다시 찾는다.
숨죽였던 기묘한 울렁거림이 어느 순간 울컥거릴 때
여행가방을 다시 꾸리고 의식처럼 필름 몇 롤을 사서.

Latte & Almond Croissant

Rainbow gelato

3rd July Sun, pm 12:33
Saint paul de vence France

Ma-r-rons in a jar

밤 껍질을 살며시 벗겨
설탕 시럽이 깊이 스며들도록
조심스럽게 담갔다 뺐다, 를
반복한다
인고의 시간을 잘 견뎌내면
말할 수 없는 흐뭇함만 남는다
매기 할머니의 마롱 글라쎄 Marron Glacé
이제 더이상 맛볼 수 없어
아련한 빈 잼병 너머

SAUCISSON
À DÉCOUPER
4,90€
TERRINE
À TARTINER
6,50€
LES SPÉCIALITÉS
MAGGI
PROFITENT À TOUT MÉNAGE

Green pistachio

헤이즐넛 크림이 어우러진
연둣빛 피스타치오가
잇새에서 아드득,
씹히던
그 순간

너를 만났다

Ocean blue truck

오렌지 블라썸 스페셜
껍질까지 담뿍 갈아 넣은
오렌지 졸임과
질 좋은 우유로 만들었다는
새하얀 셔벗
움켜쥐고는
흑녹색 눈물 흘리던 여자

20th September Mon, am 10:58
London United Kingdom

24th October Sat, pm 1:42
Barcelona Spain

12nd July Tue, am 10:05
Paris France

23rd December Sun

pm 3:02

Latte & Almond Croissant

Lemon, yellow and b...

Menu del dia

25th October Sun
pm 6:22

'Ten tins of fish, forty tins of milk, twenty pounds of powdered milk, three bottles of oil, four pots of butter, four jars of meat, two big jars of strawberries, two jars of raspberries, twenty jars of tomatoes, ten pounds of oatmeal, nine pounds of rice. That's it.'
Our supplies are holding out fairly well. All the same,

—
The diary of a young girl
Anne Frank

생선 통조림 열 개, 깡통우유
사십 개, 가루우유 이십 파운드,
기름 세 병, 버터 네 단지,
고기절임 네 통, 딸기절임
큰 병 두 개, 나무딸기는 두 병,
토마토절임 이십 병, 오트밀
십 파운드, 쌀 구 파운드
이게 전부야
우리 물자가 꽤 양호해 보이지만
찾아오는 사람도 있고
매주 먹어치우는 점을 감안하면
안심할 수만은 없어
석탄과 땔감은 충분하고
양초도 아직 넉넉해
옷 속에 숨길 수 있는
작은 지갑을 만들면
이곳을 떠나야 할 때
우리 돈을 챙겨 갈 수 있을 거야

we have to feed the office staff,
which means dipping into our reserves
every week, so it's not as much as it seems.
We have enough coal and firewood, candles too.
'Let's all make little moneybags to hide
in our clothes so we can take our money
with us if we need to leave here.'

Bloody cherries

18th June Mon
am 11:29

Temptation on way home

BIMBO
FRIGO
Cornetto
1€

BIBLIOTHEQUE
bibliothèque jeunesse
Isle Saint-Louis
heures d'ouverture
mardi, jeudi, vendredi
16h30 - 18h30
ou pendant les vacances scolaires :
13h30 - 18h30
mercredi, samedi
10h - 12h30
13h30 - 18h
GOUVERNEMENT DE VICHY,
ILS FURENT EXTERMINÉS
DANS LES CAMPS DE LA MORT.
NE LES OUBLIONS JAMAIS
mairie | quatre | paris
BABYBOURSE 0-3 ANS
les foulées du Marais
LIVE PAINTING
LA POSTE

11st October Tue

pm 4:16

Latte & Almond Croissant

Long neck, scarlet lips

내가 원하는 건 당신의
입술이에요
당신의 입은 상아로 된 탑 위에
붙은 빨간 띠 같아요
상이 칼로 두 동강 낸
석류 같기도 하고요
티레의 정원에 핀 석류꽃은
장미보다는 붉지만
당신 입술만큼 붉지는 않지요

Thy mouth is like a band of
scarlet on a tower of ivory.
It is like a pomegranate cut in
twain with a knife of ivory.
The pomegranate flowers that
blossom in the gardens of Tyre,
and are redder than roses,
are not so red.

– Salome
Oscar Wilde

장사꾼의 자존심을 걸고
말해보세요
이건 '진짜' 보석이 아닌 듯해요
자 보라구
붉은 루비는 원래
제 주인을 만났을 때여야만
빛을 발하는 거야
내 보기엔 이미 빛나기 시작했어
아가씨 손가락에서

2nd November Tue, pm 3:29
Český Krumlov Czech

Horizontal weight

KUB
KUB
BOUILLON
KUB
KUB
KUB
PAIC
Crio
PAX
PAX
Tide
Tide
2.90

깍둑 썬 버터의
농후함으로 구운
빵 오 쇼콜라 Pain au chocolat
진한 홍차나 코코아
큼직하고 두툼한 도넛, 호박파이
매콤한 진저케이크와
레몬 글레이즈를 입힌
윤기 흐르는 옥수수파운드
노랑으로 흐드러지는 작은 향연

SZTAJN
Sacha finkelsztajn
la boutique jaune
PATISSIER
DDISH SANDWICHES
www.laboutiquejaune.com
DELICATESSEN
TARAMAS
La Rose du Désert
PETIT SAINT-MARTIN
DES SOURIS ET DES HOMMES

STEREOPOSTCARDS
WITH ORIGINAL PHOTOS
98,- 3D
HAND
MADE

21st September Tue

pm 2:17

Latte & Almond Croissant

Escargots sauce d'ail

마늘 소스
달팽이

PART II
A LA CARTE

14th October Thu, pm 12:48
London United Kingdom

Follow arrow

In the town where I was born
Lived a man who sailed to sea
And he told us of his life
In the land of submarines

So we sailed up to the sun
Till we found the sea of green
And we lived beneath the waves
In our yellow submarine

– Yellow submarine
The Beatles

HIPPIES
USE
SIDE DOOR
Budweiser
BENTLEY PARKING ONLY
BMW PARKING ONLY
BSA PARKING ONLY
Corvette PARKING ONLY ALL OTHERS WILL BE CRUSHED
CITROËN PARKING ONLY ALL OTHERS WILL BE CRUSHED
INDIAN PARKING ONLY JAP BIKES WILL BE CRUSHED
JEEP PARKING ONLY ALL OTHERS WILL BE CRUSHED
JAGUAR PARKING ONLY ALL OTHERS WILL BE CRUSHED
MG PARKING ONLY
MERCEDES PARKING ONLY
MAZDA PARKING ONLY ALL OTHERS WILL BE CRUSHED
MORGAN PARKING ONLY ALL OLTHERS WILL BE TOWED
SPACE FOR MINI PARKING ONLY
MUSTANG PARKING ONLY ALL OLTHERS WILL BE TOWED
ROLLS ROYCE
RENAULT PARKING ONLY
RANGE ROVER PARKING ONLY
SPACE FOR smart
SUBARU PARKING ONLY
SUZUKI PARKING ONLY

Dandelion water

해바라기 씨 껍질을
카페 바닥에 흩뿌리며
너와 나 우리와 우리
동공이 일렁이는 저녁
고흐가 즐겨 마셨다던
싸구려 독한 술은
개미 허리와 민들레 잎사귀를
섞어놓은 맛이 났지

St Christopher's Place
St Christopher's Place
Cafe Creperie
Café Crêperie
26

Blue on the red

바스락대는 종이 봉투 속
간장 종지만큼 작은
유리병에 든 나무딸기 잼
럼주에 몸 씻어 술향기 머금은
진보랏빛 건포도 타르트
다크 초콜릿으로 감싼
수제 프랄린
한동안 기척 없던 우편함에서
남몰래 발견한 것

3rd June Tue, am 10:44
Berlin Germany

Hey, Mr. Blacks

15th December Sat, pm 2:17
Vienna Austria

Festiveness at a plaza

9th December Wed
am 11:49

Pink clouds on streets

레몬색 터키석색 라벤더색
월귤색 와인색 계피색 블루치즈색
개암나무색 닭벼슬색
베이컨 껍질색
짓이겨진 사탕수수의 꿈과
시든 연분홍빛 실타래처럼
헤어진 뒤로 이제 더이상
기억나지 않는
너의 귓불색

30th November Mon
pm 1:28

광기 품은 한 예술가는
작업에 몰두할 때 오직
후추 뿌린 빵과 물만을 먹었다네
진득한 호수와
터키석처럼 연푸른 눈동자
날쌘 고양이 한 마리가
해골 눈매 지닌 발코니 위로
지치지도 않고 넘나들었다

20th November Fri
pm 4:05

Feast of sweetness

19th June Thu
pm 3:06

Small stage for life

2nd September Wed
pm 5:14

10 DEC THU / SUNNY

Praising what is lost makes the rememberance dear

– All's well that ends well
William Shakespeare

잃어버린 것을 찬양할수록
그것에 대한 추억이
더 귀중해진다네

21 DEC FRI / SUNNY

Everyone wondered, but no one could tell, when would young oyster boy come out of his shell?

– The melancholy death of oyster boy
Tim Burton

모두가 궁금해했지만
아무도 말할 수는 없었지,
언제 그 어린 굴 소년이
그의 껍질을 깨고
나올 것인가?

우리가 감탄할 때마다 그는
더 많은 셔츠를 가져왔고,
이 부드럽고 사치스러운 언덕은
점점 더 높아만 갔다
문장이 새겨진 줄무늬 셔츠,
산홋빛의 체크무늬 셔츠,
사과빛 푸른 셔츠, 인디언 블루의
이니셜이 새겨진 라벤더빛 혹은
연한 오렌지빛의 셔츠들

그 순간 갑자기 데이지가
이상한 소리를 내며 얼굴을
셔츠 더미에 파묻고
격렬하게 울기 시작했다
"너무, 너무 아름다운 셔츠들이야"
그녀가 흐느꼈다
두터운 셔츠 더미에 파묻혀
그녀의 목소리가 띄엄띄엄
들려왔다

While we admired he brought more
and the soft rich heap mounted higher-
shirts with stripes and scrolls and plaids in coral
and apple green and lavender and faint orange
with monograms of Indian blue.
Suddenly with a strained sound Daisy bent
her head into the shirts and began to cry stormily.
"They're such beautiful shirts,"
She sobbed, her voice muffled in the thick folds.

It makes me sad because I've never seen such- such beautiful shirts before

–The great Gatsby
F. Scott Fitzgerald

"너무 슬퍼
한 번도 이렇게,
이렇게 아름다운 셔츠들은
본 적이 없거든"

8th October Thu, pm 2:49
Barcelona Spain

돌바닥 둥근 번철에서
모락모락 피어오르는
희뿌연 입김, 곱아드는 발끝
눈물만큼이나 부옇고
투명한 정어리와
지나치게 차가운 맥주
그녀들의 속눈썹 끝자락에
매캐한 밤 굽는 연기처럼
나지막히 걸리었다

I
Miserere nobis
자비를 베푸소서
Have mercy on us

14th November Sat, pm 12:21
Cadiz Spain

Her silent sigh

그녀는 보이잖는다,
안개의 엷푸른 스카프가
검은 숲과 희미한 유자빛 하늘을
가리었기에, 허나 그녀는
기다리고 있음을 안다
초조하고 차가이
흐느낌 같은 것이
싸늘한 한숨에 스며들면서

I cannot see her, since the mist's
pale scarf obscures the dark wood
and the dull orange sky;
But she's waiting, I know,
impatient and cold,
half sobs struggling into
her frosty sigh.

–A winter's tale
D. H. Lawrence

Plastic merry

8th December Tue, pm 2:37
Sevilla Spain

Crumbly afternoon

곱씹는 후회만큼이나
비릿한 생햄 여운에
나도 모르게, 그만,

파삭하게 흩날리는
메밀가루 같은 오후 햇살에
배곯은 지빠귀 하나가
볶은 보리처럼 날아들더라

15th November Sun, pm 1:45
Cadiz Spain

Rutab Mu'assal

사프란 속의
대추야자

PART。III
DESSERT DISH

그리고 제일
비밀스러운 방법으로
그는 검은 점이 박힌 파랑새의
새알 같은 것을 만들었어
이것을 입에 넣고 빨면
차츰차츰 작아져서
나중에는 분홍빛 설탕으로 된
작은 아기새가 혀끝에 앉게 되는
그런 과자도 만들었단다

– Charlie and the chocolate factory
Roald Dahl

30th November Wed
am 7:41

And, by a most secret method,
he can make lovely blue birds' eggs
with black spots on them,
and when you put one of these
in your mouth, it gradually
gets smaller and smaller until
suddenly there is nothing left
except a tiny little pink sugary
baby bird sitting on the tip
of your tongue.

Sweets
Sugar Mice
CLOSED
OPENING HOURS
WEEKDAYS 10am-4pm
WEEKENDS 11am-5ish!
CAMPBELL'S Perfect TEA

Schwoof
Wir haben für
Sie geöffnet!
* Warme Küche ab 12.30h *

Peppery man in Vienna

6th December Tue
pm 5:02

Knælende med nedadbøjet hoved
1915

Kat. 32
Blyant, akvarel og dækfarve på papir.
28,5x46cm
Sign. Forneden t.h.: EGON SCHIELE 1915
Leopold-Museum, inv. 2371

Immeasurable dream

11st July Sat
pm 1:28

Bureau de Poste
Place de
l' Hôtel de Ville
Archives Nationales
(Musée de
Centre G. POMPIDOU
Quartier du MARAIS

—

Chez la fleuriste

Jacques Prévert

Dimanche

/Sunday

Entre les rangées d'arbres de l'avenue des Gobelins
Une statue de marbre me conduit par la main
Aujourd'hui c'est dimanche les cinémas sont pleins
Les oiseaux dans les branches regardent les humains
Et la statue m'embrasse mais personne ne nous voit
Sauf un enfant eveugle qui nous montre du doigt.

DIALOGUE

필수적#유용한#식생활

FRENCH		GERMANY	
petit déjeuner	아침식사	bratwurst	구운소시지
dîner	저녁식사	frankfurter	가는소시지
l'assiette	접시	recto	차가운
café allonge	아메리카노	gemüse	채소
thé	차	eis	아이스크림
eau minéral	미네랄워터	pils	라거맥주
boeuf	쇠고기	dunkel	흑맥주
bouillon	수프	kuchen	케이크
côte	갈빗살	käse	치즈
jambon	햄	schwein	돼지
poisson	생선	hähnchen	닭
poulet	닭	hering	청어
thon	참치	frücnte	과일
oeuf	달걀	schinken	햄
champignon	버섯	brot	빵
C'est très bon	맛있어요	Danke	고맙습니다
Pardon	실례합니다	Bitte	괜찮습니다
Je suis seul	혼자입니다	Guten morgen	아침인사
L'addition	계산해주세요	Guten tag	저녁인사

RECORD

SPANISH

almuerzo	아침식사
comida	점심식사
merienda	간식
cena	저녁식사
carta	메뉴
hoy	오늘
mañana	내일
billete	표
servicio	화장실
frio	차가운
caliente	뜨거운
agua	물
hielo	얼음
mantequilla	버터
jamón	생햄
panadería	빵 가게
queso	치즈
vino rojo	레드와인
vino blanco	화이트와인

Por favor		부탁해요
Bueno		좋아요
Muy bien		아주 좋아요
Gracias		고맙습니다
Lo siento		미안합니다
Cuánto cuesta?		얼마예요?
Dónde está?		어디예요?
La cuenta		계산 해주세요
Sin sal		소금 빼주세요
uno	1	하나
dos	2	둘
tres	3	셋
cuatro	4	넷
cinco	5	다섯
seis	6	여섯
siete	7	일곱
ocho	8	여덟
nueve	9	아홉
diez	10	열

STYLE

Pass No

My first flight

to

MM DD

Meals

Own souvenir

- [ ] aisle 창가자리
- [ ] window seat 창문자리

- [ ] orange juice 오렌지주스
- [ ] sprite 탄산음료

OR

- [ ] reading 읽기
- [ ] relaxing 쉬기

- [ ] movie 영화감상
- [ ] music 음악감상

CHECKLIST

The next journey

Begins here

라떼。
아몬드 크루아상

LATTE
ALMOND
CROISSANT

인쇄 2016년 2월 11일
발행 2016년 2월 15일

저자 / 이주원
발행인 / 김수용
발행처 / 디자인소리
| 데이지북 |
서울 종로구 동숭 3길 13
02 766 7629 | daisybook.kr

www.brunch.co.kr/@vivakakao
vivakakao@gmail.com

ISBN 978-89-97613-09-0 03980
CIP 2016002200

이 도서의 국립중앙도서관 출판예정도서목록(CIP)은
서지정보유통지원시스템 홈페이지(http://seoji.nl.go.kr)와
국가자료공동목록시스템(http://nl.go.kr/kolisnet)에서
이용하실 수 있습니다.

값 12,000원

『살로메』 Salome° 기린원° 2008
오스카 와일드 Oscar Wilde
97889 439 03268

『위대한 개츠비』 The great Gatsby° 문학동네° 2010
F. 스콧 피츠제럴드 F. Scott Fitzgerald
97889 546 10469

『악마의 정원에서』 In the devil's garden° 생각의나무° 2005
스튜어트 리 앨런 Stewart Lee Allen
97889 849 83991

『The melancholy death of oyster boy』 Faber and Faber° 1998
Tim Burton
97805 712 24449

『The diary of a young girl』 Penguin classics° 2000
Anne Frank
97801 411 82759

『Charlie and the chocolate factory』 Puffin books° 2007
Roald Dahl
97801 424 10318

『Egon Schiele』 2000
Leopold museum/Wien
211 00001 00230

『Paris pastry club』 Hardie grant books° 2014
Random House Inc
97817 427 04715

BOOK
REFERENCE

내 이 세상 도처에서 쉴 곳을 찾아보았으되,
마침내 찾아낸, 책이 있는 구석방보다
나은 곳은 없더라

In omnibus requiem quaesivi,
et nusquam inveni nisi in
angulo cum libro

—Thomas à Kempis

Latte & Almond Croissant

Here is not the end